Pause & Choose

Live Deliberately

The life you inherit
is not the life you must live

NOVA KADE

vol. 1

Pause & Choose explores how automatic habits, inherited beliefs, and unexamined identities quietly shape our lives — and how awareness restores freedom.

Contents

THE PAUSE & CHOOSE MANIFESTO

Live Deliberately

Most people do not choose their lives.
They inherit them.

They inherit beliefs without examining them.
Identities without questioning them.
Values without discovering whether they are true.

This inheritance is rarely forced.
It is accepted quietly, through repetition, comfort, and the desire to belong.

Over time, habit replaces attention.
Agreement replaces understanding.
Reaction replaces choice.

This is not freedom.
It is automatic living.

Pause & Choose begins with a simple recognition:

If you didn't pause, you didn't choose.

Pause is the interruption of habit.
It is the moment when reaction is noticed instead of obeyed.

Pause does not require withdrawal or isolation.
It requires attention.

Without pause, action is automatic.
Without pause, choice is an illusion.

Choice is not preference.
It is not impulse.
It is not doing what feels easiest or most familiar.

Choice is alignment.

It is acting from what is seen clearly,
rather than from what has been inherited.

Choice requires responsibility.
And responsibility often feels uncomfortable at first.

This discomfort is not a mistake.
It is the cost of freedom.

Pause & Choose does not offer a new ideology.
It does not replace one belief system with another.

It offers something quieter, and more demanding:

The refusal to live on borrowed certainty.

Truth is not collective.
It cannot be transferred, repeated, or inherited.

It must be discovered personally,
through attention to what is actually happening—
in thought, in relationship, and in action.

To live deliberately is not to live perfectly.
Habits return.
Old patterns reappear.

The difference is simple:

You notice.

And in that noticing, choice becomes possible again.

A deliberate life is not defined by achievement,
recognition, or certainty.
It is defined by clarity.

By responding instead of reacting.
By seeing before acting.
By choosing rather than repeating.

This work is not about becoming better.
It is about becoming aware.

It does not promise comfort.
It promises honesty.

Not instruction,
but interruption.

Not answers,
but the return of responsibility.

Pause.
Choose.
Live deliberately.

Chapter One

The Comfort of the Crowd

Most people do not think for themselves.
They participate.

Participation feels active.
It feels social.
It feels responsible.

In reality, it often replaces thinking.

The crowd does not ask for clarity.
It asks for agreement.

And agreement is easier than understanding.

A weak person is rarely found alone.
He is usually found in a crowd.

Not because the crowd makes him strong,
but because it protects him from responsibility.

Thinking requires effort.
It introduces uncertainty.
It demands that one stand by what one sees.

The crowd offers something simpler: support.

Inside it, a person does not have to be right—
only reinforced.

Belonging feels like strength.
Often, it is surrender.

The crowd does not form because people are confident.
It forms because they are afraid.

Afraid of being wrong.
Afraid of standing apart.
Afraid of discovering that what they believe may not be true.

So beliefs are inherited instead of examined.
Identities are accepted instead of questioned.
Ideals are repeated instead of lived.

Over time, repetition begins to feel like truth.

It is not.
It is familiarity.

A crowd is not conscious.
It does not observe.
It reacts.

When large numbers of people begin to think alike,
praise the same figures,
and reject the same doubts,
something quiet but serious happens:

Pause disappears.

Pause & Choose

And without pause, choice follows.

Choice is a capacity.
Like any capacity, it weakens when neglected.

When generation after generation repeats the same selections—
the same beliefs,
the same loyalties,
the same explanations—
they are no longer choosing.

Choice has been outsourced.

What remains is behavior.

This is how freedom is lost.

Not through force,
but through comfort.

A society that does not question
does not need to be oppressed.
It only needs to be managed.

A familiar story.
A reassuring authority.
A shared enemy.
A sense of belonging.

The crowd complies—
not because it is evil,
but because it is tired.

People often mistake this tiredness for peace.

It is not peace.
It is numbness.

Peace requires clarity.
Clarity requires attention.
Attention requires the willingness
to stand alone—
if only for a moment.

The crowd removes that moment.

This book does not ask you to reject society or tradition.
That would be another form of escape.

It asks something quieter,
and far more difficult:

To pause.

To notice when agreement replaces understanding.
To notice when belonging replaces honesty.
To notice when comfort replaces truth.

Only then does choice return.

And with choice, freedom.

Not the loud freedom of slogans,
but the quiet freedom of a mind
that is no longer borrowed.

Chapter Two

The Inheritance of Identity

No one begins life as a blank slate.

You are born into a language you did not choose,
a culture you did not design,
a set of beliefs you did not examine,
and a history you did not live.

At first, this inheritance is simply context.
It allows orientation.
It gives structure.

Only later does it become definition.

What once surrounded you
slowly begins to describe you.

Identity arrives quietly.

A name is given.
A story is repeated.
A role is suggested.

You learn what is admired,
what is discouraged,
and what is expected.

Long before you are capable of serious questioning,
you are told who you are.

And once identity is accepted,
it begins to defend itself.

Identity does not seek truth.
It seeks continuity.

To question it feels disruptive.
To examine it feels unnecessary.
To step outside it feels risky.

So most people do not question identity at all.

They decorate it.
They strengthen it.
They pass it on.

This is how identity survives
without ever being examined.

What is often called conviction
is usually familiarity.

The mind grows comfortable
with what it hears repeatedly.

What is repeated often enough
begins to feel self-evident.

Over time, identity stops being background.
It becomes a lens.

You no longer encounter reality directly.
You encounter it as identity allows.

This is why arguments rarely change minds.

People do not defend ideas.
They defend belonging.

To challenge a belief
is to threaten continuity.

To threaten continuity
is to awaken fear.

The reaction is immediate.

Not because the challenge is wrong,
but because identity feels endangered.

Identity simplifies the world.

It creates sides.
It defines insiders and outsiders.
It tells you where you stand.

This clarity feels stabilizing.

But it comes at a cost.

Once you define yourself,
you confine yourself.

Every label limits perception.
Every allegiance narrows attention.

The world becomes smaller
even as certainty grows.

Notice how early this conditioning begins.

Children are praised for repeating correct answers,
not for asking careful questions.

They are rewarded for fitting in,
not for seeing clearly.

Understanding is secondary.
Belonging is primary.

By adulthood, this lesson feels natural.

It no longer feels taught.

Most people live their entire lives
inside this inherited structure.

They call it culture.
They call it tradition.
They call it faith.

Rarely do they call it conditioning.

Conditioning feels invisible
because it is familiar.

Like water to a fish,
identity is unnoticed
until one attempts to step outside it.

Pause & Choose

To step outside identity
is not to reject your past.

It is to stop being possessed by it.

You do not need to destroy
what shaped you.

You only need to see it clearly.

Seeing is enough
to loosen its grip.

This is where Pause & Choose
moves from idea to practice.

Pausing creates distance.
Distance creates clarity.
Clarity restores choice.

You may still belong to a culture.
You may still speak its language.
You may still participate in its rituals.

But you no longer confuse inheritance with truth.

Freedom does not mean
having no identity.

It means not being ruled by one.

It means using identity as a tool,
not living as its product.

This freedom is subtle.
It does not announce itself.

It simply stops reacting.

Most people never experience this shift.

Not because it is impossible,
but because it feels lonely at first.

And loneliness,
in a world trained to equate belonging with safety,
is often mistaken for failure.

It is not.

It is the beginning of independence.

This chapter does not ask you
to abandon who you are.

It asks a quieter,
more unsettling question:

Who are you
without what you were given?

Until this question is allowed,
life remains borrowed.

And borrowed lives—
no matter how orderly—
are never fully lived.

Chapter Three

Belief and Psychological Comfort

Belief enters life quietly.

It does not arrive as doctrine or declaration.
It settles through repetition, reassurance, and the desire for stability.

At first, belief feels helpful.
It explains.
It organizes.
It soothes.

Only later does its cost become visible.

Human beings seek certainty naturally.

Life is unpredictable.
Outcomes are uncertain.
Loss is unavoidable.

Belief offers something the world cannot guarantee:
a sense of psychological shelter.

It tells us what things mean,
why events happen,
and where we stand.

This explanation feels grounding.
Even when it is inaccurate.

Belief is powerful because it reduces anxiety.

It closes questions quickly.
It provides ready-made conclusions.
It removes the need to look too closely.

Once belief is in place,
curiosity weakens.

Not because curiosity is wrong,
but because it feels unnecessary.

This is why belief is rarely chosen deliberately.

It is absorbed.

From family.
From culture.
From authority.
From repetition.

By the time belief is noticed,
it already feels personal.

Questioning it feels intrusive.
Almost impolite.

To examine a belief
is to risk psychological exposure.

This risk is not abstract.
It is felt physically.

As tension.
As defensiveness.
As discomfort.

The body reacts
before the mind has time to reason.

Belief is not just an idea.
It is a form of safety.

Notice what happens
when a deeply held belief is questioned.

The response is rarely curiosity.

It is speed.

Arguments tighten.
Certainty hardens.
Listening disappears.

This reaction is not evidence of truth.
It is evidence of attachment.

What feels threatened is not logic,
but comfort.

Belief offers more than explanation.

It offers innocence.

If the belief is correct,
responsibility feels lighter.

You are aligned with something larger.
You are justified.
You are no longer required to look directly.

Belief absorbs doubt
before doubt becomes inquiry.

This is the hidden cost.

Belief closes attention.

Once conclusions are accepted,
questions feel unnecessary—
even dangerous.

Life becomes repetition
instead of discovery.

Meaning becomes inherited
rather than lived.

Truth behaves differently.

Truth does not reassure.
It unsettles.

It does not simplify complexity.
It exposes it.

Truth does not offer shelter.
It offers contact.

This is why truth feels uncomfortable.

Not because it is harmful,
but because it removes psychological padding.

Most people do not reject truth
because it is false.

They reject it
because it does not protect.

Belief shields the mind.
Truth engages it.

Engagement requires presence.
Presence requires effort.

Belief offers rest.

This book does not argue
that belief is immoral or ignorant.

It points to its function.

When you see clearly
what belief does for you,
its grip loosens naturally.

Not through effort.
Through understanding.

Freedom does not come
from replacing one belief with another.

That is only substitution.

Freedom appears
when the need for belief itself dissolves.

When certainty is no longer required
to face life honestly.

This dissolution does not create confusion.

It creates attentiveness.

You listen more carefully.
You react less quickly.
You become interested
in what is actually happening.

Life stops being filtered
through explanation.

Belief ends inquiry.
Attention restores it.

This is the shift
Pause & Choose points toward.

Not belief versus disbelief,
but belief versus awareness.

A life lived without psychological belief
is not empty.

It is responsive.

Action arises from observation,
not from inherited conclusions.

This does not make life easier.

It makes it real.

Belief comforts the mind.
Truth engages it.

And engagement,
even when uncomfortable,
is the beginning of freedom.

Chapter Four

The Fear of Standing Alone

Standing alone rarely begins as a decision.

It begins as a hesitation.

A pause in conversation.
A moment of doubt before agreement.
A quiet sense that something does not fully align.

At first, this hesitation feels insignificant.
It is easy to ignore.
Easier still to smooth over.

But it marks the beginning of independence.

Human beings are not designed for isolation.

We depend on one another for survival, learning, and belonging.
Connection is not weakness.
It is necessity.

But over time, the need for connection becomes entangled
with the need for agreement.

Belonging slowly replaces understanding.

To stand alone does not mean physical separation.
It means psychological independence.

It means allowing one's perception
to matter more than approval.

This shift is subtle,
but its emotional impact is strong.

The moment agreement is withheld,
distance appears.

This distance is often misinterpreted.

It is experienced as discomfort,
unease,
or fear.

Not fear of others,
but fear of losing orientation.

When you no longer fully share the group's certainty,
you are no longer sure where you stand.

This uncertainty feels destabilizing.

Belonging offers relief.

Inside a group, responsibility is distributed.
Judgment is shared.
Doubt dissolves into consensus.

To step outside this arrangement
is to carry responsibility alone.

That weight is what most people fear.

This is why people often return
to beliefs they have already outgrown.

Not because those beliefs convince them,
but because they reassure them.

Familiar explanations feel safer
than honest uncertainty.

Independence feels exposed.

The fear of standing alone
is rarely acknowledged directly.

Instead, it disguises itself.

As loyalty.
As politeness.
As practicality.
As "not wanting to make things difficult."

These justifications feel reasonable.

They are also evasions.

To stand alone is to remove buffers.

There is no group identity to hide behind.
No shared certainty to lean on.
No authority to absorb responsibility.

You meet life without intermediaries.

This contact feels raw.

Many people mistake this rawness for danger.

They interpret discomfort
as evidence that something is wrong.

So they retreat.

Agreement returns.
Belonging is restored.
Tension fades.

What fades with it is awareness.

Standing alone is not heroic.

It does not require defiance or opposition.

Often, it is almost invisible.

You speak less.
You listen more.
You pause before responding.

You do not announce disagreement.
You simply stop pretending.

This quiet honesty is unsettling to others.

Not because it attacks them,
but because it removes predictability.

The group no longer knows
how to place you.

This uncertainty creates friction.

Few relationships survive this transition unchanged.

Some deepen.
Some dissolve.

This is not punishment.

It is alignment.

What remains is no longer held together
by agreement or habit,
but by presence.

Standing alone does not mean rejecting others.

It means no longer abandoning yourself.

You may still participate.
You may still belong.

But belonging is no longer purchased
at the cost of clarity.

This chapter offers no reassurance.

Only recognition.

If discomfort arises while reading,
do not rush to escape it.

That discomfort is the fear
of standing without borrowed certainty.

When observed without avoidance,
it loosens.

To live deliberately
is not to live comfortably.

It is to live without leaning.

Without borrowed conclusions.
Without inherited direction.

This capacity —
to stand briefly, quietly, alone —
is what turns awareness
into freedom.

Chapter Five

Why Thinking Feels Dangerous

Thinking should feel natural.
For many people, it does not.

It feels tiring.
It feels uncomfortable.
Sometimes, it even feels wrong.

This discomfort is not accidental.
It is learned.

Children begin life curious.

They ask questions without concern for efficiency or correctness.
They explore without worrying about conclusions.

At first, this curiosity is tolerated.
Soon, it is directed.

Questions that slow progress are discouraged.
Questions that challenge authority are redirected.
Questions without clear answers are quietly set aside.

What is rewarded instead is correctness.

Education, in many places, does not cultivate thinking.
It trains recall.

The correct answer matters more than the careful question.
Speed matters more than depth.
Certainty matters more than understanding.

Over time, a subtle lesson is absorbed:

Thinking too much is inefficient.
Thinking differently is unsafe.

By adulthood, this lesson feels natural.

Thinking is no longer associated with discovery.
It is associated with pressure.

With judgment.
With being evaluated.
With the risk of being wrong.

So most people avoid thinking deeply
unless they are forced.

Thinking is disruptive.

A person who thinks carefully
does not move at the expected pace.

They hesitate where others comply.
They pause where others react.
They complicate what others want simplified.

This does not make them wrong.
It makes them difficult to manage.

Systems prefer predictability.

Obedience is reliable.
Repetition is efficient.
Independent thinking is neither.

So obedience is framed as discipline.
Compliance is framed as maturity.

Thinking becomes optional.
Following becomes normal.

Another reason thinking feels dangerous
is that it removes comfort.

Thinking dismantles borrowed explanations.
It exposes contradiction.
It reveals uncertainty.

For a mind trained on certainty,
this feels like collapse.

It is not collapse.
It is reorientation.

But reorientation offers no guarantees.

The mind prefers conclusions.

Conclusions allow rest.
They close effort.
They provide finality.

Thinking resists finality.

It keeps questions open.
It demands attention.
It refuses premature answers.

For the conditioned mind,
this feels threatening.

This is why people rush to opinion.

Silence feels awkward.
"I don't know" feels weak.
Pausing feels unprepared.

So opinions are adopted quickly—
often borrowed,
rarely examined.

Over time, opinion hardens into identity.

Thinking threatens identity.

When you think honestly,
you may discover that what you believe
no longer holds.

This discovery carries a cost.

You can no longer hide behind
"this is how we do things"
or
"this is what we believe."

Responsibility returns.

Most people are not afraid of thinking itself.
They are afraid of what thinking may require.

Thinking may demand change.
Change may demand loss.
Loss may demand courage.

The mind senses this chain
and resists at the very first step.

This is why thinking often begins
during disruption.

Loss.
Failure.
Crisis.
Disillusionment.

When familiar structures collapse,
thinking is no longer optional.

It becomes necessary.

But thinking does not require crisis.

It requires permission.

Permission to pause.
Permission to not conclude.
Permission to remain uncertain
without rushing to escape it.

This permission is rarely granted by society.
It must be taken.

Pause & Choose
is not a call to think more.

It is a call to think honestly.

Not defensively.
Not performatively.
Not to win.

But attentively.

To think deliberately
is to stay with what you do not yet understand.

It is to allow clarity to form
instead of forcing answers.

It is to notice
without immediately protecting identity.

Thinking feels dangerous
because it dissolves illusion
before it reveals truth.

This dissolution feels like loss
only because certainty was mistaken for stability.

True stability appears later—
after illusion loosens its grip.

This chapter does not ask you
to become intellectual.

It asks something simpler
and far more demanding:

To stop avoiding your own awareness.

When thinking is allowed
without fear of consequence,
it no longer feels dangerous.

It feels alive.

Chapter Six

The Illusion of Certainty

Certainty does not arrive loudly.

It settles quietly,
often disguised as confidence,
decisiveness,
or conviction.

At first, it feels helpful.
It brings relief.
It reduces tension.

Only later does its rigidity become visible.

Life is unstable by nature.

Outcomes change.
Circumstances shift.
Control is limited.

Certainty offers protection against this instability.

It promises something solid
in a world that does not stay still.

The mind clings to that promise.

Certainty behaves in predictable ways.

It concludes quickly.
It resists revision.
It narrows attention.

Once certainty takes hold,
curiosity weakens.

Questions feel unnecessary.
New information feels intrusive.

Thinking slows not because answers were found,
but because inquiry has been closed.

This is why certainty is attractive.

It ends discomfort efficiently.

Doubt disappears.
Ambiguity collapses.
Tension resolves.

The relief is immediate.

The cost is delayed.

Certainty divides the world cleanly.

Right and wrong.
True and false.
Us and them.

This simplicity feels stabilizing.

But reality is not clean.

Reality is layered, changing, and often contradictory.

Certainty simplifies life
by distorting it.

People often confuse certainty with clarity.

They are not the same.

Clarity expands perception.
Certainty restricts it.

Clarity adjusts when new information appears.
Certainty defends itself.

Clarity is responsive.
Certainty is rigid.

The mind prefers certainty
because uncertainty requires presence.

To live with uncertainty,
you must remain attentive.

You must listen.
You must observe.
You must tolerate not knowing.

Certainty allows withdrawal.

Once you are certain,
you can stop looking.

This withdrawal is socially rewarded.

Certain people appear confident.
They speak decisively.
They reassure others.

Uncertain people appear weak,
even when their uncertainty is honest.

So certainty is encouraged,
while attentiveness is overlooked.

Every rigid ideology
begins with a hunger for certainty.

Not a devotion to truth,
but a fear of doubt.

Once certainty hardens,
it seeks reinforcement.

Contradiction is dismissed.
Questions are treated as threats.
Dissent becomes dangerous.

This is not strength.

It is fragility protecting itself.

Understanding behaves differently.

As understanding deepens,
certainty loosens.

You begin to notice nuance.
You recognize limits.

You see complexity without panic.

This is not confusion.

It is humility.

And humility is intelligence.

Pause & Choose
does not invite uncertainty for its own sake.

It invites honesty.

To stop pretending
that certainty equals wisdom.

To admit — quietly, without shame —
"I do not yet know."

When certainty loosens,
something unexpected happens.

Attention returns.

You listen more carefully.
You react less defensively.
You adjust more easily.

Decisions stop being reactions.
They become responses.

Certainty does not collapse through argument.

It dissolves through awareness.

When you see what certainty provides —
relief, identity, reassurance —
you no longer confuse it with truth.

What remains is not chaos.

It is presence.

Presence does not promise safety.

It promises contact.

Contact with life as it is,
not as certainty insists it must be.

This contact can be uncomfortable.

It is also lighter
than living inside illusion.

This chapter completes a quiet shift.

From concluding
to observing.

From defending
to listening.

From certainty
to attention.

What follows is not confusion.

What follows is responsibility.

Chapter Seven

Truth as Personal Discovery

Truth rarely arrives through argument.

More often, it appears quietly—
in moments of attention,
in small recognitions,
in seeing something that no longer fits.

This is why truth is difficult to transmit.

It does not move easily through words.
It does not belong to groups.
It does not settle into formulas.

Truth is encountered, not accepted.

Much of what people call truth
is learned secondhand.

Someone explains it.
Someone experiences it.
Someone writes it down.

We understand the explanation,
repeat the language,
and mistake familiarity for knowing.

This is how truth becomes information.

Information is useful.
It is also safe.

Truth is neither.

Information can be stored.
Truth must be lived.

Information describes reality.
Truth alters how you relate to it.

Once something is seen clearly,
it cannot be unseen.

This change does not announce itself.
It simply makes pretense difficult.

This is why truth cannot be collective.

Groups can share beliefs.
They cannot share perception.

Fear, desire, loss, and uncertainty
are encountered individually.

No one can see on your behalf.

Any system that claims otherwise
asks for obedience, not awareness.

When people hear that truth is personal,
they often misunderstand.

They assume it means
"anything goes"
or
"nothing is real."

It does not.

Personal discovery is not arbitrary.

It requires attention,
honesty,
and the willingness to question oneself.

Truth does not arrive through effort.

It appears when attention is steady
and defenses are relaxed.

You notice a reaction repeating.
You recognize an assumption as false.
You see that a belief no longer holds.

These moments are easy to dismiss.

They are also irreversible.

Truth carries responsibility.

Once you see something clearly,
you cannot claim ignorance.

You may still choose comfort.
You may still avoid action.

But avoidance is now conscious.

This changes the nature of choice.

Truth does not elevate you.

It does not make you special.
It does not give authority.

It changes you quietly.

Reactions soften.
Certainties loosen.
Listening deepens.

Others may not notice.

You do.

This is why truth cannot be mass-produced.

The moment it is packaged,
simplified,
or turned into instruction,
it loses immediacy.

What remains may be guidance.
It may be helpful.

But it is no longer truth.

Words can point.
They cannot deliver.

At some point, language must step aside
so perception can operate directly.

This book is no exception.

If it becomes something you quote,
it has failed.

If it becomes something you notice from,
it has done its work.

Personal discovery begins simply.

Not with philosophy.
Not with analysis.

But with attention to what is happening—
in thought,
in emotion,
in relationship.

This attention has no agenda.

It does not aim to improve.
It does not try to fix.

It watches.

Most people avoid this watching
because it removes distraction.

Without distraction, patterns appear.

Reactions repeat.
Avoidances reveal themselves.
Self-deception becomes visible.

This can be uncomfortable.

Discomfort is not harm.

It is clarity arriving.

Truth does not arrive all at once.

It unfolds.

Each clear seeing restores a small freedom.

You react less automatically.
You choose more consciously.

Life does not slow externally.

It slows internally.

This is what it means
to live deliberately.

Truth as personal discovery
has no endpoint.

There is no final position to defend.
No permanent conclusion to reach.

Only increasing honesty
with what is.

This honesty requires humility.

Humility is not thinking less of yourself.
It is thinking less about yourself.

It is attention freed from self-protection.

In that freedom,
truth becomes visible—not as belief,
but as movement.

This chapter marks a transition.

From dismantling
to listening.

From borrowed meaning
to lived clarity.

What follows is not belief.

What follows is responsibility.

Chapter Eight

Responsibility and Freedom

Freedom is often imagined as relief.

Relief from rules.
Relief from pressure.
Relief from obligation.

This image makes freedom attractive.
It also makes it misleading.

Freedom is not relief.
It is ownership.

Ownership begins quietly.

It appears the moment something is seen clearly and can no longer be ignored.

A pattern is noticed.
A reaction is recognized.
An excuse loses its force.

Nothing dramatic happens.

But something irreversible has begun.

Pause & Choose

When awareness appears, responsibility follows.

Not as a command.
Not as a moral demand.

As a fact.

Once you see,
you are involved.

You may still choose comfort.
You may still avoid change.

But avoidance is no longer unconscious.

This alters the nature of choice.

Many people say they want freedom.

What they often want is escape.

Escape from decision.
Escape from consequence.
Escape from accountability.

Freedom offers none of these.

It removes hiding places.

This is why freedom feels heavy at first.

Responsibility has weight
when it has long been avoided.

But this weight is not punishment.

It is coherence.

When perception and action align,
energy returns.

When they do not,
tension accumulates.

Notice how exhausting it is
to live against what you see.

Explaining.
Justifying.
Rationalizing.

This effort consumes attention.

Responsibility simplifies.

There is less to defend.

Responsibility is often confused with burden.

A burden is imposed.
Responsibility is assumed.

A burden resists.
Responsibility responds.

When responsibility is owned willingly,
it no longer feels heavy.

It feels stabilizing.

Freedom without responsibility becomes chaos.
Responsibility without freedom becomes obedience.

Both are distortions.

They arise when freedom and responsibility
are separated.

In reality, they appear together.

You cannot have one without the other.

This is why external authority is appealing.

It promises order without awareness.
Guidance without responsibility.

Follow the rule.
Trust the system.
Obey the expert.

And if something goes wrong,
the responsibility is not yours.

Pause & Choose
dismantles this arrangement.

It does not reject learning or guidance.
It rejects substitution.

You may listen.
You may learn.
You may consult.

But you do not surrender your seeing.

Responsible freedom expresses itself quietly.

In how you speak.

In how you listen.
In how you decide.

It does not perform virtue.
It does not seek approval.

It acts because something is clear—
not because something is expected.

When responsibility is embraced,
decision-making simplifies.

You stop asking,
"What should I do?"

You begin asking,
"What is honest here?"

The answer is rarely complex.

It is often inconvenient.

A deliberate life is not optimized.

It is aligned.

Aligned with what you see.
Aligned with what you know.
Aligned with what you are willing to face.

This alignment produces strength—
not force,
not dominance,
but integrity.

Integrity is the absence of inner conflict.

It does not guarantee success.
It does not prevent loss.

It removes self-betrayal.

And that removal
creates quiet stability.

Freedom is not the absence of limits.
It is the absence of self-deception.

Responsibility is not obligation.
It is clarity in action.

Together, they form the foundation
of a life that is chosen
rather than inherited.

Chapter Nine

Action Without Ideology

Action usually feels immediate.

Something happens.
A response follows.
Little thought appears between the two.

This speed feels natural.
It also feels decisive.

But speed is not clarity.
It is habit moving quickly.

Most action is shaped before it occurs.

Beliefs suggest what matters.
Identity suggests what must be defended.
Ideology suggests what is right.

By the time action arrives,
the decision has already been made.

What follows looks like choice.
It is execution.

Ideology simplifies action.

It provides answers in advance.
It removes hesitation.
It tells you what to support
and what to oppose.

This efficiency feels empowering.

But efficiency is not attention.
It is automation.

When action is driven by ideology,
the situation itself becomes secondary.

Reality is filtered through conclusions
formed elsewhere.

The response may be forceful.
It may be confident.

It is rarely careful.

Ideology promises moral certainty.

This certainty feels stabilizing.

But moral certainty often produces blindness.

When being right matters more than seeing clearly,
harm is easily justified.

Not intentionally—
but inevitably.

Action without ideology begins differently.

It begins with pause.

You look at what is actually happening,
not what belief says should be happening.

You consider context.
You notice consequence.
You allow complexity.

Only then does action emerge.

This kind of action feels slower at first.

It does not rely on ready-made answers.
It does not rush toward expression.

But once clarity appears,
action becomes precise.

There is little inner debate.
No explanation is required.

Action without ideology is often misunderstood.

It can appear inconsistent.

One day you act one way.
Another day differently.

But inconsistency is only a problem
when identity demands continuity.

When awareness guides action,
adaptation is intelligence.

Ideological action seeks victory.

It wants to win.
To dominate.
To prove correctness.

Clear action seeks resolution.

It responds to what is needed,
not to what must be defended.

This does not mean passivity.

Action without ideology can be firm.

When something is clearly harmful,
it is addressed directly.

When something is unclear,
action is postponed.

Both require discipline.

Most systems are uncomfortable
with this kind of action.

It cannot be predicted easily.
It cannot be mobilized through slogans.
It cannot be controlled through belief.

It responds to reality,
not instruction.

To act without ideology
is to trust perception over doctrine.

It means accepting that situations differ
and answers cannot be preloaded.

There are no templates.

This exhausts a conditioned mind.

It frees an attentive one.

Action without ideology
does not make you morally superior.

It makes you responsible.

You cannot hide behind causes.
You cannot outsource conscience.

Each action is yours.
Each consequence is yours.

This responsibility sharpens attention.

You become careful,
not cautious.

Responsive,
not hesitant.

Decisive,
not rigid.

Such action rarely announces itself.

It does not perform virtue.
It does not seek validation.

It acts because action is required—
not because belief demands expression.

This is what it means
to live deliberately in the world.

Not as a follower.
Not as a rebel.

But as a person
who pauses,
sees clearly,
and acts accordingly.

Chapter Ten

Living Without Authority

Authority enters life early.

It appears as guidance,
as instruction,
as reassurance.

At first, it is practical.
Someone knows how something works.
Someone has been here before.

Trusting this guidance is sensible.

Only later does authority become something else.

There is a difference between functional authority and psychological authority.

Functional authority helps you navigate the world.

You trust a pilot to fly a plane.
A doctor to diagnose illness.
An engineer to build a bridge.

This kind of authority is specific,

limited,
and testable.

It supports intelligence.

Psychological authority is different.

It tells you what to think,
what to value,
and what is true.

It replaces observation with obedience.

Once accepted,
it relieves you of responsibility
for seeing clearly.

This relief is why it is attractive.

Most people do not seek authority because they are ignorant.

They seek it because they are tired.

Tired of uncertainty.
Tired of deciding.
Tired of holding ambiguity.

Authority promises rest.

Someone else will decide.
Someone else will know.

You only have to follow.

When psychological authority is internalized,
questioning feels unnecessary.

Even disloyal.

Obedience becomes virtue.
Doubt becomes threat.

This shift happens quietly.

No one announces it.
It simply settles in.

Living without authority
does not mean rejecting knowledge.

It means refusing substitution.

You listen.
You learn.
You consider.

But you do not surrender
your capacity to observe.

You remain responsible
for what you accept
and what you decline.

Many people mistake independence for arrogance.

They assume that questioning authority
means claiming superiority.

It does not.

It requires humility.

Because you are no longer pretending
to know what you have not seen.

Authority simplifies life.

It offers ready-made conclusions.
It reduces friction.
It stabilizes identity.

But it also freezes inquiry.

Once an answer becomes final,
attention stops.

Life turns into maintenance.

Living deliberately requires something else.

Continuous observation.

Authority seeks certainty.
Observation notices change.

Authority wants permanence.
Observation sees movement.

Where observation is alive,
authority naturally weakens.

Teachers can point.
Books can inform.
Traditions can preserve insight.

But none of them can replace seeing.

The moment they do,
they become obstacles.

Living without authority
is not rebellion.

Rebellion still depends on authority—
something to oppose.

Freedom does not oppose.

It sees.

When authority dissolves,
something unexpected happens.

You become more careful.

You no longer rush to conclusions.
You no longer borrow confidence.
You no longer hide behind consensus.

This care is not hesitation.

It is precision.

A life without psychological authority
is not chaotic.

It is grounded.

Grounded in observation.
Grounded in consequence.
Grounded in responsibility.

You act.
You observe results.
You adjust.

There is nothing to defend.

This way of living
does not produce movements.

It does not create leaders or followers.

It produces individuals.

Individuals are difficult to manage.

This is why authority is constantly promoted.

Not because it serves truth,
but because it preserves order.

This chapter does not ask you
to distrust everyone.

It asks something quieter
and more demanding:

To trust your capacity to see.

To learn without surrendering awareness.
To listen without becoming obedient.

When authority falls away,
what remains is not emptiness.

What remains is presence.

And presence—
when allowed to guide action—
is sufficient.

Chapter Eleven

Relationships Without Roles

Most relationships begin simply.

Two people meet.
They speak.
They spend time together.

At first, there is attention.

Later, something else takes shape.

Expectations appear.
Patterns settle.
Roles form.

The relationship becomes familiar.

Roles are not imposed maliciously.

They develop naturally.

Parent and child.

Partner and partner.
Teacher and student.
Leader and follower.

Each role carries assumptions about behavior,
responsibility,
and permission.

These assumptions make relationships manageable.

They also limit them.

Roles provide structure.

They tell us how to behave,
what is acceptable,
and what is expected.

This structure reduces uncertainty.

But it replaces meeting with performance.

You are no longer responding to the person.
You are responding to the role.

From early life, this conditioning is reinforced.

Approval is linked to obedience.
Affection is tied to meeting expectations.
Belonging becomes conditional.

Over time, this feels normal.

Love becomes transactional.
Listening becomes selective.
Silence becomes threatening.

Most conflict in relationships
does not arise from disagreement.

It arises from violated expectation.

Someone does not behave as the role requires.
Someone steps outside the script.

This feels like betrayal
because the relationship was never free to begin with.

Roles protect identity.

If I know who I am supposed to be,
I know how to act.

This certainty feels stabilizing.

But it is fragile.

The moment the role is questioned,
the self feels threatened.

So roles are defended—
often unconsciously.

This is why honesty feels risky.

Honesty disrupts roles.
It introduces unpredictability.

To say what you actually feel
is to risk misunderstanding,
disapproval,
or loss.

So most people edit themselves.

They speak carefully.
They listen strategically.
They perform.

Over time, relationships become tiring.

Not because closeness is demanding,
but because pretense is.

Maintaining a role requires effort.

You must remember who you are meant to be
and who the other expects you to be.

This distance quietly erodes intimacy.

A relationship without roles begins with attention.

You meet the other person
as they are now—
not as they were,
not as they should be.

You allow change.

This is unsettling,
because change threatens continuity.

In role-based relationships,
continuity is valued over truth.

In honest relationships,
truth is valued over stability.

This does not mean cruelty.

It means clarity.

To relate without roles
is to drop psychological protection.

You do not hide behind identity.
You do not speak from obligation.
You do not demand consistency.

You listen
without rehearsing your response.

This kind of listening is rare.

Relationships without roles
cannot be guaranteed.

Some connections deepen.
Others dissolve.

This is not failure.

It is alignment.

What remains is no longer held together
by agreement or habit,
but by presence.

Most people fear this way of relating
because it removes control.

You cannot manage someone
who is free to change.

So control is disguised as care.
Expectation is disguised as love.

This disguise is convincing.

It is also damaging.

Love does not require sameness.

It does not say,
"Remain as you were."

It says,
"Be honest about who you are becoming."

Relationships without roles are quieter.

There is less performance.
Less explanation.
Less defense.

There is more listening.
More space.
More truth.

They are not dramatic.

They are alive.

This chapter does not offer an ideal.

It describes a possibility.

A way of meeting another person
without ownership,
without performance,
without fear.

Few relationships survive this transition unchanged.

Those that do
become something else entirely.

When roles fall away,
what remains is not chaos.

What remains is contact.

And contact—
when allowed without interference—
is enough.

Chapter Twelve

A Life That Is Chosen

A deliberate life is rarely dramatic.

It does not announce itself.
It does not seek validation.
It does not require recognition.

It simply unfolds differently.

By now, something may already feel quieter.

The pull of the crowd is weaker.
Identity feels less solid.
Belief feels less necessary.
Certainty feels less convincing.
Authority feels less central.

What remains may feel unfamiliar.

This unfamiliarity is not loss.

It is space.

A life that is chosen begins in this space.

Not with new answers,
but with a different relationship to questions.

Questions are no longer problems to be solved quickly.
They become signals for attention.

You stop rushing toward conclusions.
You allow understanding to form.

Choosing does not mean constant decision-making.

It means awareness.

You notice when you are reacting.
You notice when you are repeating.
You notice when you are borrowing.

In that noticing,
choice returns naturally.

A chosen life is not free of habit.

Patterns return.
Old tendencies reappear.
Comfort remains tempting.

The difference is simple:

You see it.

And seeing changes your relationship
to what is happening.

Responsibility no longer feels imposed.

It no longer feels heavy,
because it is no longer resisted.

You respond because something is clear,
not because something is expected.

Action becomes quieter.
More precise.
Less defensive.

Relationships shift.

You no longer require constant agreement.
You no longer need to be understood at all costs.
You no longer shape yourself
to preserve familiarity.

Some connections fall away.
Others deepen.

You stop holding together
what no longer aligns.

Work changes as well.

Success is no longer measured by comparison.
Failure is no longer defined by shame.

You do what is clear.
You stop when it is not.

There is dignity in this simplicity.

A chosen life is not heroic.

It does not aim for greatness.
It does not seek moral superiority.

It values honesty over admiration.
Clarity over comfort.

It accepts that misunderstanding
is sometimes unavoidable.

This way of living cannot be taught.

It can only be recognised.

Words may point.
Practices may support.

But the work happens
in ordinary moments—

when you pause before agreeing,
when you stop repeating what no longer fits,
when you act without borrowed certainty.

Pause & Choose
is not a method.

It is a stance.

A willingness to interrupt habit
before it becomes action.

A willingness to see
before deciding.

There is no final state.

No arrival.

A chosen life is renewed continuously.

Each pause restores choice.
Each choice restores freedom.

If this book has done anything,
let it be this:

Not to give you something to believe,
but to return you to your own seeing.

Not to tell you how to live,
but to remind you that living
is not inherited.

It is chosen.

Pause.
Choose.
Live deliberately.

About the Writer

Nova Kade is a writer and applied philosopher exploring how deliberate pauses transform the way we think, decide, and live. Through the Pause & Choose series, Nova develops philosophy not as theory, but as a daily practice—one rooted in presence, clarity, and conscious choice.

www.ingramcontent.com/pod-product-compliance
Ingram Content Group UK Ltd.
Pitfield, Milton Keynes, MK11 3LW, UK
UKHW021400190726
13845UKWH00028B/792

9 789356 265738